LEADING COUNSEL

Vol. 2

Spotlights on Top Elder Law and Estate Planning Attorneys

LEADING ELDER LAW AND ESTATE PLANNING ATTORNEYS

FEATURING:

Richard Tizzano
Meg Pauken
Stephanie Keating
Peggy Hoyt
Robert Pecori
Kimberly Foulk
Ryan Wilson

Remarkable Press™

Royalties from the retail sales of **"LEADING COUNSEL VOLUME 2: SPOTLIGHTS ON TOP ELDER LAW AND ESTATE PLANNING ATTORNEYS"** are donated to the Global Autism Project:

AUTISM KNOWS NO BORDERS;
FORTUNATELY NEITHER DO WE.®

The Global Autism Project 501(C)3 is a nonprofit organization that provides training to local individuals in evidence-based practice for individuals with autism.

The Global Autism Project believes that every child has the ability to learn, and their potential should not be limited by geographical bounds.

The Global Autism Project seeks to eliminate the disparity in service provision seen around the world by providing high-quality training to individuals providing services in their local community. This training is made sustainable through regular training trips and contiguous remote training.

You can learn more about the Global Autism Project and make direct donations by visiting **GlobalAutismProject.org.**

Copyright © 2021 Remarkable Press™

All rights reserved. No part of this publication may be reproduced, distributed, or transmitted in any form or by any means, including photocopying, recording, or other electronic or mechanical methods, without the prior written, dated, and signed permission of the authors and publisher, except as provided by the United States of America copyright law.

The information presented in this book represents the views of the author as of the date of publication. The author reserves the right to alter and update their opinions based on new conditions. This book is for informational purposes only.

The author and the publisher do not accept any responsibilities for any liabilities resulting from the use of this information. While every attempt has been made to verify the information provided here, the author and the publisher cannot assume any responsibility for errors, inaccuracies, or omissions. Any similarities with people or facts are unintentional.

Leading Counsel Volume 2/ Mark Imperial —1st ed.
Managing Editor/ Shannon Buritz

ISBN: 978-1-954757-10-3

LEADING COUNSEL

Vol. 2

CONTENTS

A NOTE TO THE READER

Thank you for obtaining your copy of "LEADING COUNSEL VOLUME 2: Spotlights on Top Elder Law and Estate Planning Attorneys." This book was originally created as a series of live interviews; that's why it reads like a series of conversations, rather than a traditional book that talks at you.

My team and I have personally invited these Attorneys to share their knowledge because they have demonstrated that they are true advocates for the success of their clients and have shown their great ability to educate the public on the topic of Elder Law and Estate Planning.

I wanted you to feel as though the participants and I are talking with you, much like a close friend or relative, and felt that creating the material this way would make it easier for you to grasp the topics and put them to use quickly, rather than wading through hundreds of pages.

So relax, grab a pen and paper, take notes, and get ready to learn some fascinating insights from our Leading Counsel.

Warmest regards,

Mark Imperial
Publisher, Author, and Radio Personality

INTRODUCTION

"LEADING COUNSEL VOLUME 2: Spotlights on Top Elder Law and Estate Planning Attorneys" is a collaborative book series featuring leading professionals from across the country.

Remarkable Press™ would like to extend a heartfelt thank you to all participants who took the time to submit their chapter and offer their support in becoming ambassadors for this project.

100% of the royalties from this book's retail sales will be donated to the Global Autism Project. Should you want to make a direct donation, visit their website at GlobalAutismProject.org

RICHARD TIZZANO

CONVERSATION WITH RICHARD TIZZANO

> ***Richard, you are an estate planning attorney from Washington. Tell us about your practice and the people you help.***

Richard Tizzano: I have been an estate planning attorney for over 30 years. In 2000, my father required long-term care and was moved into a nursing home. I realized then that I had no real clue about how the long-term care process worked. I was helping clients with estate planning day after day, but I realized I wasn't giving my clients the opportunity to think about aging and how that might look or how they might need to plan for long-term care. That is when I decided to expand my estate planning practice to include the necessary perspective of helping clients address those issues involving aging.

> ***What are the consequences of not planning for aging?***

Richard Tizzano: I have discovered that if you don't plan, you will likely end up in a crisis which dramatically reduces the quality and number of options that will be available. These issues of long-term care planning are going to come up eventually. In my book, "Accidental Safari," I wrote about the "circle of life;" at the beginning of life, we need someone to hold us, feed us, love us, and change our diapers. If we live long enough, we will eventually need someone to do those things for us again. If we avoid thinking about it, we avoid dealing with it and planning for it. As I said, sooner or later, these issues will have to be addressed if we live long enough. If I can guide clients to consider their preferences and inform them how to put a plan in place, I can help change their future.

> ***What documents are essential in the planning process?***

Richard Tizzano: When we think about estate planning, most people think about the Last Will and Testament.

While the Will is important and addresses the issues concerning the handling of our remains and our financial and personal possessions, the Will only has power after we die. By far, the most important documents we need while we are alive are the Powers of Attorney for Finance and Health Care and a Living Will. These documents authorize a person or persons to step in to assist you when you can no longer make decisions for yourself. As I said earlier, if we fail to plan for the possibility that we will, at some point, need care and help with the tasks of daily living, we will end up in crisis. Taking the time to plan now will save lots of time, money, stress, and grief later on.

Additionally, in Washington State, we can prepare a Living Will, which is called an "Advance Health Directive to Physicians." The Directive informs the individual(s) you named in your Power of Attorney for Health Care of your wishes for end-of-life care in the event that you can no longer communicate your wishes. Those persons you trust and appoint in your Medical Power of Attorney are thereby authorized to assert your Directive to Physicians when needed.

Are there any myths or misconceptions you would like to address?

Richard Tizzano: I have never met anyone who is confused about the fact that we can't "take it with us." A U-Haul doesn't follow the hearse. Every one of us will leave it behind, whatever "it" is. But, if we do some proper planning, we can make a difference with the things we leave behind. I encourage my clients to ask themselves, "What can I do *now*?" In reality, people usually take more time planning their next vacation or which refrigerator to buy than they do thinking about their estate plan. It can really benefit you and your family if you take the time to plan ahead. Planning can make a difference.

What does the planning process look like? Where should people begin?

Richard Tizzano: I recommend that people do a little research before they sit down to plan. I offer free educational estate planning seminars online, and my book "Accidental Safari" is another good place to begin. Alternatively, you can jump in and make an appointment with an Elder Law attorney to ask questions and start the thinking process. A typical cycle would look like this: a new client comes to see me, we begin with an information-gathering time when they tell me about themselves, their lives, and their needs. I ask questions to help the clients identify their needs and preferences. I explain the various options for them to consider based on their particular situation and the issues they have explained to me.

Often people become paralyzed by fear because they don't understand their options. They are afraid they'll make a choice only to discover later that they could have done something more, or better, for a loved one. So they do nothing for fear of making a poor choice, which hurts everyone in the end. Education is essential to combat the fear of making a wrong decision. Understanding the options gives people confidence. You may still be losing a person you love, but at least you will have confidence that you did everything that you could and made the best decision possible given the options available.

Once all of the cards are on the table with a new client, I think it's important for me to give them some hope and inspiration. I find that it's helpful to them when they can accept that they're doing the best they can under the circumstances and making the most preparation for the future. Ultimately, our faith will give hope and encouragement that things are going to be okay. It takes courage for people to acknowledge they are moving to the next phase of their lives. Perhaps they are willing to sell the big house and downsize or move into an assisted living facility, rather than waiting for a crisis to push them into that when they have made no preparation. The options decrease if we wait for the crisis to act. But, if you have the courage to take a step forward, you will find many more options and opportunities.

> ***What inspired you to get started in elder law and estate planning?***

Richard Tizzano: My journey began when I was 12 years old. My mother had a stroke that left her paralyzed. My father and I cared for her for the rest of her life, which she spent in a wheelchair. Many years later, I attended law school and began a practice in estate planning. The experience that really pushed me toward elder law was seeing my father become unable to care for himself about 25 years ago. It was challenging to figure out what the options were and how the system worked. The Medicare/Medicaid process was instituted in 1965, which gave rise to the nursing home industry. Under the law, you could build a nursing home, fill it with people, and when the individual could no longer pay for their care, the government would pay for care. This revolutionized how we provided care for our seniors. And in some ways, it is sad. But at least the option is there; the opportunity is there. There are Medicaid benefits, VA benefits, long-term care insurance, and various other resources for people who need care and need financial assistance to pay for it. It is comforting for people to know that there are options and ways to deal with these issues.

> ***How can people connect with you and learn more?***

Richard Tizzano: My website is www.accidentalsafari.com. "Accidental Safari" is the title of the book I wrote to provide help for people who are navigating the challenges that come with aging. I'm always eager to advance awareness of these issues and the options available to meet them by speaking whenever I can. Education is essential, and the book or my online seminars are great places to start.

RICHARD TIZZANO

Attorney
Sherrard McGonagle Tizzano & Lind

Richard C. Tizzano is a principal at Sherrard McGonagle Tizzano & Lind. He has 30+ years of legal experience in Washington and California and the United States District Court for the Western District of Washington. Richard specializes in Elder Law and Long-Term Care Crisis Management, Strategic Care Cost Risk Mitigation and Sustainability, Estate Planning & Settlement, Guardianships, and Adoptions.

Richard is a graduate of Vanguard University of Southern California and Seattle University School of Law. Prior to law school, Richard served as an ordained Minister with the Assemblies of God Church and has extensive experience in both the financial and commercial real estate markets. This unique background enables him to provide a compassionate, comprehensive approach to his law and estate planning practices.

ACCIDENTAL SAFARI, by Richard C. Tizzano

Richard Tizzano wants to take you on a journey. Perhaps a safari. As an expert in elder law & estate planning, Richard knows the routes and the forks in the road. The safari metaphor is the theme for his new book, ACCIDENTAL SAFARI, a guide for navigating the challenges that come with aging. With over 30 years of offering experience, compassion, and insight into the lives of others, Richard is uniquely qualified to write this book.

WEBSITE:

www.accidentalsafari.com

PHONE:

360-779-5551

EMAIL:

richardt@westsoundlegal.com

FACEBOOK:

https://www.facebook.com/pg/AccidentalSafariOfficial/posts/

LINKEDIN:

https://www.linkedin.com/in/richard-tizzano-18353a5

MEG PAUKEN

CONVERSATION WITH MEG PAUKEN

> ***Meg, you are an elder law attorney in Cleveland, Ohio. Tell us about your practice and the people you help.***

Meg Pauken: Elder law is a subset of estate planning specifically focused on addressing the issues that come up as a person ages. I typically work with families to preserve their assets so that if long-term care services are needed, an entire life's savings isn't drained. I also help people with qualifying and applying for Medicaid and planning for incapacity. At that point, another person will need to take over the day-to-day management of their affairs, and they will need the proper tools to do that. I also do regular estate planning for clients, such as wills and trusts. My goal with each client is to identify the potential problems that could occur and then create a plan to deal with those potential problems. Every client's situation is unique, and my approach is flexible, depending upon what the client needs and wants.

It is really common for adult children to call me when they notice a parent starting to "slip." I educate them and share the types of tools that I can prepare so that they will be able to manage both finances and healthcare for that parent. Sometimes, I even meet with the whole family so that everyone is on the same page.

Other times, the older adults approach me on their own. Maybe one spouse cares for the other and is worried about what will happen if they get sick. Who will care for the other spouse? They may be worried because their kids aren't local, so who can help in an emergency? Sometimes my clients need guidance about selecting a care facility or home caregiver or information about other services that might be available. I am very attuned to situations that might be dangerous for an older person or where they might be being taken advantage of.

I have worked with multiple generations of the same families, too, which is really rewarding. Adult kids will come to me because they are worried about their parents. Once we have gotten the planning done for their parents, they realize they need to do their own planning. Then, when their children turn 18, they need their own powers of attorney and health directives. I really enjoy having ongoing relationships with my clients.

When is the right time to start planning?

Meg Pauken: Over 10,000 people turn 65 every day in the United States. And that will continue through about 2030 when the entire Baby Boomer generation will be over 65. So we're experiencing this great graying of America. This will put a very big burden on the children and loved ones of this aging population, who will ultimately be responsible for caring for them. There is a real tension between the need to plan and the natural difficulty of seeing your world narrow and getting used to the idea of giving up control. I help clients and their families work through those emotions to make smart decisions for the future. There is a sweet spot where you can see how your life may play out, you're aware of chronic illnesses or possible outcomes, but you still have the cognitive ability to do the planning. I usually start to have these conversations with clients when they're about 65 to 70, but I can still help families with proactive planning up to the end of life.

What are the consequences of not planning properly?

Meg Pauken: Seeing an elder law attorney is essential, as opposed to someone who just does typical estate planning because elder law attorneys are specifically attuned to the unique issues that come along with aging. It's not theoretical to us; it is practical. When I create documents for people, I'm thinking about what tools they will need to have in place to manage expected and unexpected crises. For example, if an older person falls and ends up in the emergency room, things can start to decline rather quickly. My goal is to give my clients tools so that the person they select as their agent can manage both their health and finances, either temporarily or permanently. The power of attorney documents that I draft allow my client's agent to plan for asset transfer, apply for Medicaid, protect their spouse, manage assets, and do end-of-life planning. This is very different from a routine power of attorney drafted by a general estate planning attorney.

What are some of the most common questions you hear from clients?

Meg Pauken: Most often, clients focus on how assets will be divided after someone passes away. I bring them back to the present and say, "If something happened tomorrow and you were incapacitated but not deceased, do you have a plan in place to deal with that?" I think that's where one of the biggest misconceptions is: people believe estate planning is only for after you die. I always tell people that in my office, we plan for three phases. We plan for right now, for when you are incapacitated and for after you pass away. People tend to forget about that middle zone of incapacity because they don't want to think about it, but it is critical because it will give your family the ability to help you when (or if) that happens. Unless you work with an attorney to create the proper documents, your family will be left scrambling to manage. They may even have to go to court to get a guardianship, which is expensive and time-consuming.

Family members often think that if a parent or spouse has begun to have memory issues, they can no longer do the planning, which is not necessarily true.

The other common questions I get are about Medicaid. Clients think they have too much money to qualify or think it is too late to protect assets. There is nearly always a way to protect at least some of their assets, and it is rarely too late - provided the proper tools are in place.

> ***Can estate planning and elder law be handled with one attorney?***

Meg Pauken: Most elder law attorneys are very well equipped to do estate planning. I nearly always do estate planning along with the elder planning for my clients. If you are a very high net worth individual, you may want to deal with a combination of the two. Some elder law attorneys have sufficient training to deal with high net worth individuals who may have estate tax issues, while some don't. If you know your estate is likely to be taxable (right now, that is $11.5 million), you might want to get some additional advice from a tax attorney.

> ***How do you start the conversation about planning with a loved one?***

Meg Pauken: Having that conversation is interesting. Often, as an outsider of the family, I can ask really blunt questions of dad, while the children can't. I can look at him across the table and say, “How will you know when it is time to stop driving?” as opposed to the children saying, “Dad, give us your keys!” Just getting your loved one in the attorney’s door under the estate planning banner is an opportunity to open the conversation. I can guide the discussion to the issues of capacity and planning for incapacity once I have the client at the table.

I recommend that adult children be direct. Maybe use the situation of a friend or family member whose parent has recently gotten ill to open the door to ask if mom or dad has a healthcare power of attorney or advance directives, for example.

Also, there is a nonprofit called “ The Conversation Project” for families having difficulty with these conversations. If you Google it, you will find sample scripts, journals, and conversation topics to help open the door to communication. It is a great resource.

What is it like to work with you?

Meg Pauken: My firm is very focused on educating our clients while treating them compassionately and with respect. We work with a wide variety of clients from different backgrounds, and it is important to me that they are all treated with dignity.

Our usual process is to have an initial meeting to discuss the situation, which might last an hour to an hour and a half. We send potential clients a questionnaire to complete in advance to get a picture of their family situation, their finances, and what planning they may have already done. At that first meeting, I educate them about potential issues and how we might plan for them. I will tell them what I recommend and how much my fee will be.

We charge flat fees for planning so that there are no surprises and so that clients feel free to ask as many questions as they need to without worrying about a big bill.

Once a client has decided to move forward, we will draft documents or complete an analysis and a plan to qualify for Medicaid. We will meet again, usually by Zoom, to go over the plan. I really focus on educating my clients so that the plans and documents I prepare don't just sit on a shelf. I want them to understand and be able to use the tools I create for them. Once they are satisfied with the documents, we schedule a time to sign them. If the client is not local to me, I will send them the documents with instructions for signing, but I prefer to do it in my office to make sure it's done correctly.

If a client cannot come to my office for health reasons, I can go to them, although I have to charge a bit more for that service.

Once everything is completed, we create a document binder with instructions and an emergency contact card. We also give them access to digital copies of everything through our secure portal. I will continue to answer their questions, and I follow up at least once a year to see how everything is working for them.

It is a little different for Medicaid application cases because there are more steps to the process, but we maintain the same focus on education, compassion, and respect.

What inspired you to get started in elder law?

Meg Pauken: I had done estate planning as part of my practice almost since I started as a lawyer, and then I walked with my parents through the end of their lives and saw how the documents I drafted would actually be used in real life. My dad had been the caregiver for my mom, who had dementia, and then he started to decline. My dad was the strong, independent patriarch of the family who began to lose his abilities, so I dealt firsthand with that scenario. I know how hard it is to watch a loved one decline physically and mentally. Watching them go through this opened my eyes to many of the pitfalls that can happen if you have not done the proper planning and don't have the right tools in place.

I really like working with older people. I like their stories, and I enjoy talking with them. I think it is important that as people age, they are able to make their own choices and plans, rather than having a court or some other person make decisions for them. Sometimes that means that I ask their kids to leave the room while we discuss sensitive issues. Sometimes it means that I help them navigate tense family relationships. What is important to me is that they feel respected and treated compassionately and with dignity. I truly love what I do.

Is there anything else you would like to share?

Meg Pauken: One of the key issues for families is spotting that "golden window" of opportunity. When someone first gets a diagnosis of Parkinson's disease or early-onset Alzheimer's, or other similar illnesses, you've got a window where you can still do effective planning, but it can shut quickly. People need to be aware of that and act accordingly.

The other thing is, don't be afraid to reach out to an elder law attorney for a consultation. It can be overwhelming to deal with aging parents or an ailing spouse. An elder law attorney can educate you and point you toward resources you might not be aware of. They can help you put together a plan to deal with your situation. I can almost guarantee that you will feel less anxious after talking with them, and the consultation cost is usually pretty reasonable. Elder law attorneys want to educate and help - it's what we do.

> ***How can people connect with you and learn more?***

Meg Pauken: My website is www.paukenlegal.com. I have a contact page on my website where you can book an appointment directly. Although I am physically located in the eastern suburbs of Cleveland, Ohio, my practice is statewide. My office phone number is 440-468-0003. You can also easily find me by Googling "Meg Pauken."

MEG PAUKEN

Attorney/Founder
Pauken Legal Services LLC

Meg Pauken is the owner of Pauken Legal Services LLC, in Chagrin Falls, Ohio. Her practice focuses on Elder Law, Estate Planning, and Special Needs Planning. She draws on over 25 years of experience to provide wise and compassionate counsel, helping her clients plan for the protection and distribution of their assets and the care of themselves and their families. Meg's goal with every client is to identify potential problems and create individual solutions to deal with those potential problems. She is a member of the Ohio Bar Association, the Cleveland Metropolitan Bar Association, the Geauga County Bar Association, the National Academy of Elder Law Attorneys, and ElderCounsel. She is a frequent speaker and writer on topics related to Elder Law and Estate Planning. Ms. Pauken earned a BA from Miami University and a JD from Case Western Reserve School of Law.

WEBSITE:

www.paukenlegal.com

PHONE:

440-468-0003

EMAIL:

Meg@paukenlegal.com

FACEBOOK:

https://www.facebook.com/PaukenLegal

LINKEDIN:

https://www.linkedin.com/in/meg-pauken-8923804/

STEPHANIE KEATING

CONVERSATION WITH STEPHANIE KEATING

Stephanie, you are an attorney representing New York and New Jersey. Tell us about your practice and the people you help.

Stephanie Keating: Our firm specializes in trusts, estates, and elder law. We assist our clients in planning their estates, wills, trusts, power of attorney, and health care proxies, whether it's for asset protection or estate tax planning. We also assist in elder planning, which includes long-term care planning and Medicaid applications.

What are the consequences of not planning?

Stephanie Keating: As far as the elder law arena, if you don't plan, there are only three ways to pay for your care; with your own funds out of pocket, with long-term care insurance, or with the assistance of a government benefit like Medicaid. You have to do certain things within a specific time because the government does "look backs" on particular transfers. So the sooner you do your planning, the better off you will be. Most people in this country don't have the money to pay for everything out of pocket, especially in New York, where the cost of care is high.

Also, many people are unaware that if you don't have documents like a will in place, certain things go by statute, and it may not be what you want. If you don't have a will, there is a statute that determines who gets your assets. For example, if you are married with children, the law in New York says it must be split between your spouse and your kids. If you're not married, the statute might say that it will go to siblings you don't even talk to. You certainly want to address these issues and have a say in where your assets go. Also, how are you going to pay your taxes? Certain assets should pay for their own taxes, while others should not. Finally, if you have minor children, who will be the Guardian? These are among the most important reasons to start the planning process.

> ***How has the pandemic affected your area of practice?***

Stephanie Keating: The pandemic really raised the issues of health care directives, powers of attorney, and wills. Your agents in your health care directives can speak for you when you can no longer speak for yourself. So you want to name people you are comfortable giving that responsibility to. The pandemic has brought to light the discussions that people need to have with their loved ones as far as what they want and don't want. It has also made people realize the need for power of attorney if someone was incapacitated for some time and needed a family member or friend to pay their bills or sell their property. If you don't have power of attorney in place, you could need a guardianship which is much more expensive and drawn out.

God forbid something happens to someone; a will should be in place to make sure assets go to the right people. Somebody with a child under the age of 18 needs to name a guardian through a will. Otherwise, the court decides. So people really started thinking about many of these issues due to the pandemic, and we were pretty busy for a while. There was a sense of urgency. But we got it done and continue to help people even as the pandemic slows down.

What are the first steps with a new client?

Stephanie Keating: We start the consultation with a conversation about who their loved ones are and what assets they have. What's the value? How are they titled? Do you have beneficiary designations? All of those things are important. The beneficiary designations on a retirement account would supersede any direction you have in a will, which is crucial for transfer and income tax planning reasons. What is important to you? What are your goals? Do you want to plan for long-term care? Are we potentially doing some elder law planning with the thought of Medicaid in the future? If it is a younger couple, perhaps they need to put guardians in place for their children. Older couples might be concerned about all the tax law changes being kicked around in Congress. They potentially would want to shelter and create some trusts for estate tax planning reasons. The needs of each client are unique depending on their age and goals. We tailor a plan that is best suited for the individual.

What inspired you to get started in elder law and estate planning?

Stephanie Keating: It's interesting. I am a CPA as well. So my undergraduate and initial work were in the area of accounting. Then I got interested in the world of law, specifically tax law, and went to law school after that. So the first and still the only law firm I've ever worked with specializes in trusts and estates. My two partners are also CPA attorneys. So our practice is such a specialty in that area. It was a natural progression and a great fit. I love the area of trusts and estates. I love the ability to help people who are at the worst times of their lives. Either somebody is really sick or has just lost a loved one and faces all of these problems. So we help guide them through the process from the beginning to the end with high-touch service to take the pressure off. It inspires me to know I have done something good.

When is the best time to start planning?

Stephanie Keating: Call me now. The sooner, the better. The more time we have to plan for you, the more options will be available. There is usually a good reason to have a plan no matter where you are in life. If you have young children, you want to name a guardian. If you are in your 50s, 60s, or 70s, you want to do some elder law planning. And depending on your wealth, you might want to do some estate tax planning. If you haven't revisited your will in the last three to five years, you should pick it up and look at it. And if you haven't done one at all, there's no time like the present.

> ***How can people connect with you and learn more?***

Stephanie Keating: Our firm is Schwartz, Fang & Keating. Our phone number is 516-488-0100, and we have offices in Long Island in Woodbury, NY, in Manhattan, NY, and in Edison, NJ. I'm licensed in New York and New Jersey. You can find us on the web at www.inheritlawyers.com.

STEPHANIE KEATING

Attorney
Schwartz, Fang & Keating, P.C.

Stephanie M. Keating, Esq. CPA is a partner at the law firm of Schwartz, Fang & Keating, P.C., with offices on Long Island in Woodbury, NY, in Manhattan, NY, and in Edison, NJ. Her areas of focus are Elder Law,

Estate Planning, and Estate Administration. She is an Attorney-at-Law, and a Certified Public Accountant licensed to practice in both professions in the states of New York and New Jersey.

She counsels clients on a broad range of issues, including elder law planning, estate planning and related tax work, estate and trust administration, along with tax and succession planning for family corporations and partnerships. She works closely with various clients, including entrepreneurs, corporate executives, and real estate developers, to help them identify their objectives and provide constructive solutions to meet their specific goals.

When she is not advising clients, Stephanie loves spending time with her husband Mike and their son Brian in their hometown of Williston Park, New York, and taking camping trips to new places in the U.S.

WEBSITE:
www.inheritlawyers.com

PHONE:
516-488-0100

EMAIL:
skeating@sfkesq.com

LINKEDIN:
https://www.linkedin.com/in/stephanie-m-keating-590bb914/

PEGGY HOYT

CONVERSATION WITH PEGGY HOYT

> ***Peggy, you are an attorney representing Central Florida, specifically in the Orlando area. Tell us about your practice and the people you help.***

Peggy Hoyt: We like to help people who love their families, first and foremost. We counsel people about their estate planning on a typical day, including wills, trusts, financial powers of attorney, and healthcare directives. We also help families make legal and financial decisions related to long-term care that may include in-home care, assisted living, or nursing home care. We prefer to do preventative planning but find we are experts at crisis planning when a family waits too long to begin the planning process. Our firm motto is "Partners in planning, friends for life."

I also enjoy working in specialty areas of practice, including assisting families with special needs, planning for unmarried couples, creating estate plans for pets, and cryonics estate planning.

Our firm is also available to assist families when they've lost a loved one and need to do a probate or trust administration. The laws can be complex, and we feel our job is to teach people the questions they didn't even know they needed to ask.

> ***Has the recent pandemic made people aware of the importance of planning?***

Peggy Hoyt: Absolutely. We are busier than we have ever been. I think it's a combination of things. Existing clients are doing a better job of keeping their plans updated. And, there is a steady stream of new clients who are finally getting around to doing their planning and now recognize there is no time like the present to plan. I think our mortality is a little more real for people today. More people appreciate that our time is short and life can happen fast.

I believe we are overly optimistic as a society. When asked, we generally respond, "If I die," and "When I win the lottery." Reality is very different. Most of our clients will never win the lottery, but all will certainly die.

What are the consequences of not planning?

Peggy Hoyt: The worst thing that can happen is you pass away without a plan, either a Last Will or a Living Trust. The number one thing everybody needs to have is a Last Will and Testament because if you don't have a plan, the state where you live has created one for you. And it is likely not the kind of estate plan you were expecting. There can be some really unexpected results, such as assets passing to an estranged spouse or children or properties passing in a way that requires the asset to be sold and the proceeds distributed.

For example, I have a family where the husband passed away in a third marriage situation. We are representing the surviving spouse from the third marriage, and we also have to interact with children from the first, second, and third marriages. Some of these children were adopted by the deceased, and some were adopted by others after a divorce. So there have been some very interesting outcomes that could have been planned for and avoided. Unexpected events, frustrations, and expenses keep coming up because he didn't take the time to create a Last Will.

Our goal is to help clients create "estate plans that work." This means when a person dies, there are no unexpected results, family members remain harmonious, and the estate is administered efficiently.

Is a Last Will enough? Or do people need more than that to avoid probate?

Peggy Hoyt: Actually, having a Last Will guarantees probate. Many people are not aware of this. Probate is the legal process of proving someone's will. However, I'm always the first to say that I don't think probate is a four-letter word. It just happens to be a process you go through to ensure that the deceased's last wishes are carried out. It's a court-administered process, and it's typically three overarching steps. Step one is to identify and gather the assets of the person who has died. Step two is to identify and pay the person's creditors, including filing final tax returns. And finally, step three is to distribute the assets to the intended beneficiaries.

Many people will still say they would rather not go through the probate process. In fact, they will take elaborate steps to avoid probate and, in the process, actually cause more problems. A Last Will only governs those assets that an individual owns. Jointly owned property and assets with designated beneficiaries usually avoid the probate process but can place vulnerable individuals in harm's way or have unintended consequences.

Having a Living Trust is one way to avoid probate, but ultimately, it doesn't avoid the administration process. Things still need to be done when a person dies to make sure their assets, debts, and beneficiaries are appropriately handled. So, I think it's important to have a good, long conversation with a legal professional about your goals and how to accomplish those best.

> ***You have expertise in something very unique called "cryonics." What is cryonics planning?***

Peggy Hoyt: Cryonics estate planning is aimed at individuals who want to be frozen or cryonically-preserved when they die. The expectation is that someday there will be medical technology to revive them from that preserved state and return them to full life and health. It's a very small group of clients with this particular goal, but the numbers are growing. Along with co-author Rudi Hoffman, we recently released the *Cryonics Estate Planning Handbook - Maybe You Can Take It With You.*

> ***I understand you also are passionate about estate planning for pets?***

Peggy Hoyt: This is one of my primary passions. I have no two-legged kids. I am a pet mom to horses, dogs, and cats. I call them my "children who wear fur coats." As a result, I understand how important it is to know that my pets will have forever homes if something happens to me.

Today, all 50 states and the District of Columbia have pet trust statutes. This allows pet parents to create a trust for the benefit of their loved pets, whether it is a cat, dog, horse, or other loved animal. Every day I work with clients to accomplish the goal of ensuring their loved pets stay in loving homes. You can get more information by reading my book; *All My Children Wear Fur Coats - How to Create a Legacy for Your Pet.* In addition, I host a weekly podcast of the same name, and I've founded a charity, Animal Care Trust USA, Inc., to provide pet parents with access to education and resources for protecting their pets.

What are some common myths and misconceptions about planning?

Peggy Hoyt: Everybody has an estate, whether they think they do or not. If you have even $1, that's your estate. If you have a vehicle when you pass away, that vehicle is part of your estate. If you own real property, it's part of your estate. I don't care if you are 18 or 80 years old; you need an estate plan.

Another myth is that you only need to plan for when you die. But you have a much greater likelihood of becoming mentally disabled during your lifetime than simply just passing away. So financial powers of attorney, healthcare powers of attorney, and living wills (your expression of how you want to be cared for at the end of your lifetime) are essential parts of a comprehensive estate plan. For younger people, we offer a "kids in college" plan designed for young adults that focuses on what happens if they become disabled as a result of an accident or illness so that parents and siblings can help make important decisions without the requirement of a court-ordered guardianship.

Another misconception is that estate planning is a DIY project or that all attorneys are qualified to create an effective estate plan. Estate planning is highly complex, and this area of the law is impacted by many other areas, including divorce law, real property law, guardianship law, tax law, probate and trust administration law, and contract law, just to name a few. It is nearly impossible for a layperson or an attorney without significant experience in this area to anticipate all of the potential pitfalls.

> ***What inspired you to get started in elder law and estate planning?***

Peggy Hoyt: Interestingly, as I began my professional career, I was employed as a financial consultant. In that role, I worked with many estate planning attorneys educating clients about the importance of planning and protecting their loved ones. One day, I said, "Gee, I'd really like to be an estate planning attorney." Eventually, I decided to go to law school, and I knew from the start I would focus my efforts on estate planning. My elder law interest came along a little later after my law partner was called to active duty in Iraq. He had a very busy elder law practice, and I wanted to keep his practice thriving. As a result, I learned elder law and discovered how valuable this area of practice is to families challenged by long-term care decisions. Then, my partner, Randy Bryan, and I became Florida Bar Board Certified

Specialists in Wills, Trusts, and Estates and Elder Law. Today we hold the distinction of Florida's only law firm with two individuals with these credentials.

> ***What is the first step for people who don't know where to start when planning?***

Peggy Hoyt: The first thing is educating yourself about estate planning basics and then finding a legal professional who you really like and who will teach you the questions you didn't know you needed to ask. An excellent resource can be found at www.estateplanning.com. You can locate lawyers all over the country that are members of an organization called *WealthCounsel.* If you need an elder law attorney, you can find one through *ElderCounsel.* Also, ask your friends, trusted financial advisors, or your CPA for recommendations for qualified estate planning or elder law attorneys that would be a good fit for you. Then, talk to them to find out if you are comfortable and feel they will represent your best interests. Bring all of your financial and legal documentation with you. Expect to enjoy the journey and learn a lot as part of the process.

How can people connect with you and learn more?

Peggy Hoyt: We are on the web at www.HoytBryan.com. Our phone number is 407-977-8080. We continuously offer complimentary education workshops that are available by Zoom or online. We're happy to help anyone who might need our assistance.

PEGGY HOYT

Attorney
The Law Offices of Hoyt & Bryan, LLC

Peggy is a lifelong animal advocate, pet mom, and attorney. Before entering law school, her work experience includes time as a college recruiter, financial consultant, account executive, and chief financial officer. She is a founding partner of The Law Offices of Hoyt & Bryan. Peggy is dual board certified by the Florida Bar in Wills, Trusts, and Estates and Elder Law. She is the founder of Animal Care Trust USA, Inc., a national nonprofit whose mission is to keep loved pets in loving homes by educating pet parents about the importance of pet trusts.

She practices in the areas of family wealth and legacy counseling, including trust and estate planning and administration, elder law, small business creation, succession and exit planning, real estate transactions, and animal law. In addition to her law degree, she holds a Florida real estate license. Peggy formerly held an NASD Series 7 license and life, health, and variable annuities licenses. She serves as a certified FINRA Arbitrator. Peggy was an adjunct professor of Animal Law with Barry University College of Law.

Peggy is the author of *All My Children Wear Fur Coats – How to Leave a Legacy to Your Pet*, an informative guide for pet owners who want to include their pets as part of their estate plans. She has co-authored numerous other titles, including *Special People, Special Planning – Creating a Safe Legal Haven for Families with Special Needs*;

Loving Without a License – An Estate Planning Survival Guide for Unmarried Couples and Same Sex Partners; *A Matter of Trust – The Importance of Personal Instructions*; *Women in Transition – Navigating the Legal and Financial Challenges in Your Life; Like a Library Burning – Sharing and Saving a Lifetime of Stories; Thank Everybody for Everything! Grow your Life and Your Business with Gratitude; Gratitude Expressions - a Five Year Journal; Straight Talk! About Estate Planning; Straight Talk! What to Do When Someone Dies; What's the Deal With...Estate Planning* and *What's the Deal With...Estate Administration.* Her newest book with Rudi Hoffman addresses the estate planning concerns of cryonicists and is called, *The Cryonics Estate Planning Handbook - Maybe You Can Take it With You.*

Peggy frequently speaks on estate planning and elder law topics, including pet planning and planning for families with special needs. She has been featured on CNN Financial News, in the Wall Street Journal, and the Orlando Sentinel for her dedication to pet planning. She is also highly regarded for her workshops on gratitude marketing, life balance, and law office management. She hosts a weekly "Pawcast" called *All My Children Wear Fur Coats,* available on Buzzsprout.

Her educational background includes a B.B.A (Marketing/ Management 1981), *cum laude* and M.B.A. (Finance 1982) from Stetson University. She received her law degree (J.D.

1983), *cum laude* from Stetson University College of Law. She is a member of numerous state and national organizations, including WealthCounsel and ElderCounsel, the Central Florida Estate Planning Council, the National Association of Elder Law Attorneys (NAELA), and the Academy of Florida Elder Law Attorneys (AFELA). She is active with The Florida Bar serving as a Past Chair for both the Solo and Small Firm Section and Animal Law Section. She is a member of the Elder Law Section and Real Property, Probate, and Trust Law Section.

WEBSITE:

www.HoytBryan.com

PHONE:

407-977-8080

EMAIL:

Peggy@HoytBryan.com

FACEBOOK:

https://www.facebook.com/HoytandBryan

https://www.facebook.com/AnimalCareTrustUSA

LINKEDIN:

https://www.linkedin.com/in/peggyrhoyt/

ROBERT PECORI

CONVERSATION WITH ROBERT PECORI

Robert, you are an elder law and estate planning attorney from Pittsburgh, Pennsylvania. Tell us about your practice and the people you help.

Robert Pecori: As an elder law and estate planning lawyer, I help people plan for their futures and protect their assets for the next generation. I usually deal with seniors and the disabled with elder law, and these folks often need nursing home care. There is specific planning that I can do to help these folks save their money and still get the care that they need.

Estate planning clients range from young to old, single to blended families, and also those with special needs. Many special needs individuals receive some form of government benefits to help them. To preserve those benefits, the planning for these folks must be unique. Such a plan usually consists of a Special Needs Trust.

> ***So elder law is a separate area of law from estate planning?***

Robert Pecori: Yes, elder law is a specialized area of law that deals with the unique issues seniors, the disabled, and their families face. Those issues can vary from estate planning, long-term care planning, special needs planning, Medicaid planning, Veteran's benefits, and coordination of other government benefits and insurance. Estate planning is certainly a part of planning for these folks, but they require more, and that is where the need for an elder law lawyer arises.

> ***What are the most common challenges your clients face?***

Robert Pecori: The most common challenge is paying for long-term care. Most families have no idea how expensive long-term care is until they are faced with the need, and they are usually shocked to learn that it is $10,000 a month per person on average in Western Pennsylvania. A very common phone call I receive is, "My mom fell and broke her hip. She is in rehab, and they are telling me it is unsafe for her to come home.

She must now live in a nursing home. She has a house and money in the bank. Is she going to lose those assets?" The answer is "no." An elder law attorney can help preserve those assets, save them for the next generation, perhaps transfer them to a loved one and get mom eligible for Medicaid to pay for her long-term care. Most families cannot absorb a six-figure cost per year. It is financially devastating to them. This is where an elder law lawyer can really help.

> ***How do people end up in this crisis mode? Are there things they could have done earlier to better prepare for these situations?***

Robert Pecori: Yes, you can plan well in advance of a long-term care crisis. But to be honest, most people do not. And I don't necessarily blame them. Nobody wants to go to a nursing home or think they will ever need to be in one. Even if you planned for your estate and have a will or a trust, you don't necessarily think about the long-term care component until it happens to a friend, family member, or is right on your doorstep. Then you have to deal with it. An elder law attorney, however, can help you plan well in advance of ever needing care. They can help you save money and preserve your assets for your loved ones. This type of planning may be utilizing an asset protection trust, one of the new types of long-term care insurance policies called a hybrid policy or, sometimes, both.

I often bring up the topic of long-term care when somebody comes in to talk to me about estate planning. When I'm going over their information, I say, "Look, you have obviously worked hard and done a great job growing a really nice estate here. I am happy to put estate planning documents together for you but keep in mind, the greatest threat to your assets as you age is the threat of long-term care costs. There are things that we can do right now to avoid this but even if you wait, always talk to an elder law lawyer if you are ever faced with the need for nursing home care." I've made it my mission to get the word out about elder care planning. I do in-person seminars on the topic when I can and, since Covid, I have recorded my presentation so anyone can watch it on my website. The key takeaway is don't think you just have to start writing checks to a nursing home. Always talk to an elder law lawyer if you or a loved one need long-term care.

Is having a will enough? Or do people need more than that?

Robert Pecori: It is a start, but they definitely need more. Actually, you would be amazed at how many people have no estate planning at all, and it can really cause problems. For example, if you do not have a Will, a statute determines who gets your assets upon your death. It is called the Intestacy statute. Now, it may name the people that you would have chosen, but who knows? I have a friend who died several years ago. He had talked to me about doing some planning but never followed through. He died unexpectedly. He was a lifelong bachelor with no kids and no siblings. He left a two million dollar estate that was inherited by his distant aunts, uncles, and cousins. His significant other got nothing. Is that the plan that he would have put in place? Probably not.

Also, when you ask, "Do people need more than that?" Yes, they do. The lack of a power of attorney is also a problem. I had a recent case where a single lady in her 60's became very ill. She was unconscious and in the ICU. She had a mortgage and bills due, and she had no financial power of attorney. Her brother came to me looking for help. I had to file an emergency guardian petition to have him appointed to access her funds and pay her bills. Guardianship proceedings are difficult, time-consuming, and expensive. They are best avoided and can be if a person just has a financial power of attorney.

With estate planning, there are basic documents that everyone should have: a will, financial power of attorney, healthcare power of attorney, and living will. This is an estate plan that everyone needs, regardless of age. For those with more needs or substantial assets, they need these documents and more.

With more wealth comes the need for more wealth protection, both for you and your heirs. This usually means Trust planning of some type. A common Trust is a Revocable Living Trust. This Trust holds your assets while you are alive as well as when you are gone if necessary. This Trust also avoids the probate process when you die, which is often very helpful and makes the administration of your estate easier on your heirs.

Another fairly common Trust that I mentioned earlier is a Special Needs Trust. This is a Trust used when you have a loved one who has special needs and receives government benefits like Medicaid or Social Security disability. If such a person receives an inheritance, it will disqualify them from receiving the benefits. However, if a Special Needs Trust holds their inheritance, they remain eligible for the benefits, and the trust can supplement their needs.

Other trusts that can be helpful are Asset Protection Trusts used in long-term care planning and Retirement Plan Trusts, which are beneficial to protect your retirement funds flowing to your spouse or kids. A Retirement Plan Trust, for instance, can protect your hard-earned retirement funds from your kids' divorce or bankruptcy.

> ***What myths and misconceptions exist in your area of practice?***

Robert Pecori: We just talked about a misconception; people think they don't need estate planning or perhaps only a Will. For a myth? People are often surprised to learn that Medicare does not pay for long-term care in a nursing home. Medicare is health insurance. As long as you are receiving health care, Medicare will pay. But if you get to the point where you also need long-term nursing home care, that adds room and board. Medicare doesn't pay for room and board. As we discussed earlier, this is the moment when families learn just how expensive long-term nursing home care is. I know I keep coming back to this but call an elder law lawyer right away if this happens to you or a loved one. They can almost always save assets and get Medicaid coverage for the person who needs the care.

Unfortunately, another closely related misconception here in Pennsylvania is that children are usually shocked to learn that they are responsible for their parents' care if they need long-term care and cannot afford it. This is called filial responsibility. Nursing homes can actually sue children if mom or dad need care and run out of money, and, even worse, they can pick and choose which child to come after. This is usually the child with the deepest pockets so the nursing home can be assured of collecting. This is obviously quite a scary proposition for children, but it can be avoided if mom and dad plan accordingly well in advance or, here it is again, talk to an elder law lawyer right away if care is needed.

> ***What inspired you to be a lawyer, and how did you end up focusing on elder law? How did you get started?***

Robert Pecori: Two things. Number one, I'm a third-generation lawyer. My grandfather founded our firm in 1940. Since my grandfather and father were lawyers, I always wanted to be like them. Number two, I really enjoy helping people. I get personal satisfaction from solving problems for people, saving them money, or helping them through difficult times.

The elder law component is interesting because I did my first elder law case before I realized it. My mother-in-law became quite ill years ago. My wife and I were faced with a situation where she couldn't go home and had to go to a nursing home. I had to learn on the fly and deal with her assets, get her eligible for Medicaid, and get her into a place where she could receive the care that she needed. That experience started my journey into elder law.

I have been doing estate planning for 28 years now. My grandfather was an estate planning and probate lawyer, and he taught me much of that business. My father, who I still practice with, has always done civil litigation, and I have experience there as well. Elder law wasn't even a term when my grandfather was practicing. It is a relatively new field and has become more prominent and important with our increasingly aging population. There is an existing elderly population, but it is growing quickly with the addition of the baby boomer generation, many of whom are now retirement age or older. The need for care and long-term care is just becoming greater and greater.

I always tell my clients that there is good news and bad news with our aging population: the good news is that medical science continues to make advances daily, so we have our loved ones longer. The bad news is that they likely will need more care at the end of their life, which usually means long-term care. So the need for elder law lawyers and elder care planning is getting greater and greater.

What should people look for when choosing an elder law attorney?

Robert Pecori: First, make sure you talk to an actual elder law lawyer. You want someone who is experienced in elder law and elder care planning. Many excellent estate planning lawyers are out there, but not every estate planning lawyer is an elder law lawyer. Estate planning lawyers can help you with most planning and probate work, but when an elder law issue comes up, such as filing a Medicaid application or advanced long-term care planning, you need an experienced elder law attorney. Most of us belong to the National Association of Elder Law Attorneys. If you go to naela.org, you can find an elder law lawyer in your area.

> ***How can people find you, connect with you, and learn more?***

Robert Pecori: Please visit my website: pecorielderlaw.com. You can learn more about elder law, watch my free webinar about saving your home and assets from nursing home care, and book a free consultation with me. Also, most recently, I have a new YouTube channel where I answer questions about elder law issues. You can find that link on my website as well.

ROBERT PECORI

Elder Law and Estate Planning Attorney
Pecori and Pecori Attorneys at Law

Robert Pecori is a third-generation Elder Law Attorney at Pecori & Pecori, a family firm his grandfather founded in 1940. For over 28 years, Robert has been helping families in Pennsylvania and West Virginia plan for their futures and preserve their assets. He also takes particular pride in using care and compassion to guide families through the probate process after the death of a loved one.

Robert has previously been recognized as one of Pittsburgh's finest Elder Law attorneys and was recently chosen as a "neighborhood favorite" in his community on the social media app Nextdoor. He was born and raised in Pittsburgh and received his Bachelor's Degree from Duquesne University and his Law Degree from the University of Pittsburgh.

Outside of the office, Robert is an avid biker and has been racing sports cars for more than 20 years. He and his wife also enjoy traveling. They live in the suburbs of Pittsburgh with four rescue cats who run their house.

WEBSITE:

www.pecorielderlaw.com

PHONE:

412 788-2000

EMAIL:

rpecori@pecorilawyers.com

FACEBOOK:

facebook.com/Pecori-Pecori-Attorneys-at-Law-252630507184

INSTAGRAM:

instagram.com/pittsburghelderlaw/

TWITTER:

https://twitter.com/elderlawpittsb1

KIMBERLY FOULK

CONVERSATION WITH KIMBERLY FOULK

Kimberly, you are an estate planning and elder law attorney in northwest Pennsylvania. Tell us about your practice and the people you help.

Kimberly Foulk: I have worked at Cressman Erde Ferguson for about seven years now, five of which were spent as the primary estate planning and elder law paralegal. Once I was licensed to practice law, I was fortunate to remain with CEF as an attorney. My primary practice areas are Elder Law, Estate Planning, Estate Administration, and Special Needs Planning. I am able to serve a variety of clients, from the very young who need a simple Will and Power of Attorney to the aging adults who need complex irrevocable trust and asset protection planning. I also serve clients whose loved ones have passed away and need assistance with estate administration.

Most of my clients are aging adults who are either trying to plan ahead for asset protection should they ever require skilled nursing home care or clients who have already entered the nursing home and need assistance with post-admission asset protection. I can assist clients with the entire aging continuum from when they are at home and healthy through nursing home admission planning.

What is the number one challenge your clients face?

Kimberly Foulk: The number one challenge, especially during post-admission planning, is the protection of assets. The most common question I am asked is, "How can I protect my assets from being consumed by the cost of my care at the nursing home?" Our motto here is build, protect, preserve. Build an estate plan that meets your needs today and sets the stage for success in the future, protect your assets with irrevocable trust planning, and then preserve that wealth through post-admission crisis planning.

One of the most important things you can do to ward off this challenge is to engage in estate planning before your health declines to the point where you need nursing home care. Even if you never need care in a skilled nursing facility, it's incredibly important to make sure you have engaged in planning that ensures a seamless transfer of assets to your heirs.

There is planning that should be done before your health starts to decline. For instance, making sure you and your loved ones have a Last Will and Testament, a Healthcare Power of Attorney, and Financial Power of Attorney are some of the most simple, cost-effective things you can do to plan for the future. As you age, implementing an irrevocable trust can help with the protection of assets should you ever require skilled nursing home care.

> ***What are some common misconceptions in your field of practice?***

Kimberly Foulk: My clients' biggest misconception is that the nursing home will take their house. And I can assure you, nursing homes are not in the business of trying to take your house. Another big misconception is that you have to impoverish yourself to pay for your care before you qualify for the public benefits system to assist with the payment for your cost of care.

Skilled nursing home care is very expensive. In Northwest Pennsylvania, where I practice, the monthly cost of skilled nursing home care ranges from approximately $7,000 to $10,000 per month, depending on where you live and the level of care you need. At that cost, most people will burn through their savings pretty quickly. As an elder law attorney, I can help clients preserve their assets and leverage the public benefits system. Based on the current laws in place, I can help protect almost 100% of the assets for a married couple, and for a single person, I can help protect about 50%-60% of their assets. We protect assets using various tools if a person wants to leverage the public benefits system to assist with paying for their cost of care.

Medicaid Long Term Care (MA-LTC) is the public benefits system most people will turn to if they require skilled nursing home care. This is a means-tested public benefits system which means your financial eligibility depends on your assets and income. To qualify, you can only have so many financial resources available to you. Not all resources are countable, however. You can qualify for MA-LTC and still own your primary residence, one vehicle, and prepaid burial reserves. These are what we call exempt resources.

Most people get confused about their house being "taken" when it is subject to estate recovery. If you receive

MA-LTC during your lifetime, the Commonwealth of Pennsylvania, Department of Human Services is entitled to place a lien against your probate estate to recoup funds that have been paid out during your lifetime. Essentially, if you receive MA-LTC to pay for your skilled nursing home care, and own your primary residence solely in your name when you pass away, someone will need to go through the probate process to dispose of your residence. That means your loved ones might have to sell your house when you pass away to pay back the lien imposed against your estate.

The good news is that I can help you with all of this! One of my roles as an elder law attorney is to help guide you through this process. I work with you to achieve eligibility while protecting your assets and avoiding estate recovery.

Are there mistakes that people make before coming to see you?

Kimberly Foulk: One of the most common mistakes I see is what we call "unintentional gifting." A person, or their family, recognizes that their health is failing, and they will need nursing home care. To protect assets, I see individuals start transferring resources to their children. People think, "I transferred my house to my daughter for $1; that's not a gift; she just bought it for $1." That's not *exactly* how it works. For MA-LTC purposes, that is considered a gift. The term gift has a very broad definition for Medicaid purposes. It means giving assets away for less than fair market value, making assets joint with another person, transferring assets to a trust, or having unaccounted for funds by writing checks to "cash." This situation also arises when a person operates primarily in cash. I have seen an individual take $500 a week out at the ATM and use that money to buy groceries or gas, and every month there's $2,000 that we can't account for to the County Assistance Office. Even though that person didn't give their money away, it could cause a gifting issue because we can't prove to the County Assistance Office that you didn't give that money away.

Applying for MA-LTC is essentially a financial audit of the last five years of your life. Most people have heard the term "5-year look-back rule." The County Assistance Office looks back five years to see if you have engaged in any gifting as part of the eligibility process. If you have engaged in gifting, you are penalized. The penalty means you have to privately pay for your care before Medicaid starts to pick up the tab. You can see how this could cause problems if you have given away your money and now have a penalty you need to pay through.

By engaging the services of an elder law attorney to guide you through this process, we can help you avoid some of these issues. Even better, we can help you engage in some *intentional* gifts to protect your assets and plan ahead for the penalty period that would follow.

> ***What solutions can you offer people who are in crisis mode?***

Kimberly Foulk: Post-crisis planning typically involves an aging adult who has entered a skilled nursing facility and has not engaged in any planning before entering the facility. We can help the aging adult protect their assets to preserve them for their family while also qualifying for Medicaid Long-Term Care. We leverage the public benefits system to help pay for care through what can be described as math manipulation. We take the five-year look-back rule, and we use it to our benefit. We cause intentional penalty periods by gifting. It sounds crazy, but I promise it works; this is what we do as elder law attorneys!

Here is a general idea of how this works - a single person enters a skilled nursing facility and has $100,000. This person won't qualify for MA-LTC care until their assets are reduced below a certain level. For this client, we'll say it's $2,400. So instead of spending through that $100,000 until we get down to $2,400 and then qualifying for Medicaid, we will intentionally gift some of that away to their child. Giving that money away will cause a penalty period, so we are careful not to give it all away. Since we are only giving away about half of the money, we will take the other half and use it to fund a Medicaid-compliant annuity. When combined with their other income (social security or pension), that annuity pays for their cost of care each month with a small monthly deficit. The deficit is paid from the gifted funds, and at the end of the penalty period, Medicaid begins paying for their care. This is a very simplified version of what we do but gives you a general idea of how post-crisis planning works.

Instead of this person burning through all their money before they qualify for MA-LTC, we have protected about half of their money and helped them achieve eligibility. It's so important for clients to have a Power of Attorney to engage in this type of asset protection, though. This type of planning can be done without a Power of Attorney, but it is much more difficult and costly because your loved one will likely need to seek guardianship over your estate.

There are also things you can do as far as pre-admission planning. Perhaps a client comes in, and they are in their 60s and in good health with no diagnosis of cognitive decline. They want to know how to protect their assets if they require skilled nursing home care in the future. This type of client is usually a good candidate for irrevocable trust planning. We know based on what we have discussed so far that transferring assets to a trust can cause a penalty period, but if you put those assets into a trust and don't need nursing home care for five years, even if we go five years and one day, those assets are no longer considered countable resources for eligibility purposes; we've protected them. We have also created a non-probate situation for when you pass away, saving your family time and money.

> ***What inspired you to get started in estate planning and elder law?***

Kimberly Foulk: About 15 years ago, I was working as a paralegal in a different area of law, and I really enjoyed the work. That job actually inspired me to go back to school to finish my bachelor's degree. I worked in that firm for about six years, and then I started working as an elder law and estate planning paralegal at Cressman Erde Ferguson. After about five or six years of this type of work, I really felt like I could do more. I wasn't feeling fulfilled in my career, and I saw a need in the community for this type of specialty practice.

At that point in our community, we only had two elder law attorneys, one of whom I was working for. While I was putting myself through law school, one of the elder law attorneys in the community retired, and we were down to one elder law attorney in the entire county. So we had this community of 80,000 people, and we had one elder law attorney, and I thought, "We can do better!" It's such an underserved and vulnerable area of the population; I wanted to do more for them.

While I was still working as a paralegal, I put myself through law school. I was fortunate enough to join the only American Bar Association-approved hybrid program, so I didn't have to relocate. I could stay where I was, keep working, and keep learning. When I finished law school, I was fortunate enough to stay with the same practice as an elder law attorney and fill some of that gap in our community.

> ***What should people consider when choosing an elder law and estate planning attorney?***

Kimberly Foulk: Choosing the right elder law attorney is incredibly important and sometimes a daunting task. One way to find a trustworthy attorney would be to talk to family and friends or admission staff at the nursing home for recommendations. I spend quite a bit of time connecting with local nursing homes and partnering for speaking engagements to educate the local community. I believe in empowering clients to make informed decisions by sharing information on a public platform.

Another excellent way to find an elder law attorney in your area is through the National Academy of Elder Law Attorneys (NAELA) or a local state chapter in your area. I practice in Pennsylvania, so we have the Pennsylvania Association of Elder Law Attorneys (PAELA). Those are both excellent resources to find attorneys in your area that focus on elder law and estate planning because these attorneys are usually intimately familiar with the laws of Medicaid. It's such a complex area of law, and you should use an attorney who knows the Medicaid rules and uses them daily. Also, don't hesitate to ask questions. You are retaining an attorney to protect your assets, so you should be interviewing them just as much as they interview you.

How can people find you, connect with you, and learn more?

Kimberly Foulk: Our website is www.cressmanerdelaw.com. You can call and ask for me at 814-807-1071. I'm happy to talk with you for three minutes, 20 minutes, or three hours to make sure your family is in the best position they can be in for estate planning.

KIMBERLY FOULK

Elder Law and Estate Planning Attorney
Cressman Erde Ferguson

Kimberly S. Foulk, Esquire, graduated Magna Cum Laude from Hodges University in 2016 with a B.S. in Legal Studies and from Mitchell Hamline School of Law in 2019. She was admitted to practice law in the Commonwealth of Pennsylvania in 2020. The primary focus of her practice is Elder Law, Estate Planning, Estate Administration, and Special Needs Planning.

Kimberly is a member of the Pennsylvania Association of Elder Law Attorneys (PAELA) and the National Academy of Elder Law Attorneys (NAELA). She is a frequent presenter of continuing legal education programs to other attorneys, including *How Trusts Affect Medicaid Eligibility* (NBI 2021) and *Estate and Trust Administration* (NBI 2021). She was a 2020-21 participant in the Leadership Meadville program sponsored by the Meadville-Western Crawford County Chamber of Commerce and is the Chairperson of the board for Junior Achievement of Crawford County.

Kimberly has worked at Cressman Erde Ferguson since 2014, acting as the primary estate planning and elder law paralegal. She attended law school while working full time at Cressman Erde Ferguson, graduating from the first ABA-approved hybrid in-person and online law school. She has extensive experience working with elder law and estate planning and brings a thoughtful and sophisticated approach to complicated issues for many families. Unique to her practice is her approach to Medicaid planning, where she clearly identifies the client's goals, then structures a plan that achieves the client's articulated goals, start to finish. She acts as a responsive and personable point of contact for her clients, creating accountability amid the natural complexity of Long-Term Care planning.

WEBSITE:

www.cressmanerdelaw.com

PHONE:

814-807-1071

RYAN WILSON

CONVERSATION WITH RYAN WILSON

Ryan, you are an elder law attorney and the founder of The Law Office of T. Ryan Wilson. Tell us about your practice and the people you help.

Ryan Wilson: My practice as an elder law attorney encompasses a broad spectrum of issues. I work with clients to develop legacy plans that provide for their own long-term care. I also make sure clients have the legal documents, called powers of attorney, in place so that families can help their older loved ones with financial and healthcare decisions. When clients come because their loved one didn't have the appropriate documents in place, we help them obtain legal authority to assist their loved one. I help clients plan for long-term care. Finally, we help families transfer assets after their loved one transitions. So, the themes that run through my elder law practice are assisting clients in getting the care they need and preserving family wealth.

What are some of the most common problems or challenges your clients face?

Ryan Wilson: The common challenges my clients face begin with having an older loved one in need of long-term care. This can be complicated when their loved one hasn't planned how to pay for that care ahead of time. Another challenge happens when the loved one's legal documents don't allow the families to conduct the financial transactions necessary to pay for care and preserve family wealth.

I often work with clients whose older loved one is in physical or cognitive decline. The family has gotten to the point where they know it is unsafe for their declining loved one to continue living in their home by themselves. The loved one either needs or will soon need round-the-clock nursing care. First, how do we get them care, and second, how do we pay for it? So, we could be helping the client certify the need for the care - getting the proper documents to the right people. Then, we are helping the client plan for and arrange payment for the care. This includes spending down and transferring assets consistent with the rules to provide care and preserve assets.

The process is more complicated without a well-drafted power of attorney in place. Sometimes, my client's loved one has no power of attorney at all. Other times, the client's loved one does have a power of attorney in place, but the power of attorney doesn't cover all the necessary transactions.

> ***How do you advise people to prepare so that a health crisis does not catch them off guard?***

Ryan Wilson: There are a few things people can do. First of all, get your powers of attorney in place so that someone can take care of you if you become incapacitated without having to involve the legal process. Secondly, get your powers of attorney in place, and lastly, *get your powers of attorney in place!* You really should also talk to an elder law attorney who would know specific powers that a power of attorney should contain to avoid a guardianship. A guardianship is a court proceeding in which the court finds that you cannot make decisions on your own and appoints someone else to make them for you. There are two other things people should do. First, people should plan to finance their own long-term care needs. Many of us will need professional care at some point. Finally, people should execute legacy planning documents that carry out their plans.

Do you find that your work is part therapy?

Ryan Wilson: There are definitely times when I feel like I'm part therapist. I regularly work with families under emotional stress. Seeing your loved one in decline is hard emotionally. For example, I had a client recently who had made a promise to their dad that they'd never put him in a nursing home, but the family got to a point where they could no longer manage dad's care on their own. He needed round-the-clock nursing home care. Part of being a caregiver is knowing when you can no longer manage your loved one's care without professional nursing help. In a situation like this, I am there for my clients emotionally and giving them legal advice.

What inspired you to get into elder law? How did you get started?

Ryan Wilson: Well, I had a circuitous route to it. I worked for a decade for an organization that advocates on behalf of older people, and I worked to protect older people as they saved for retirement. I developed a passion for helping people age well. When it came time for the next phase of my career, I wanted to help people age well, protect their families, and have a personal relationship with the people I help. My experience made the transition to a new chapter easier for me. I really enjoy working with my clients.

> ***How can people find you, connect with you, and learn more?***

Ryan Wilson: My website is www.ryanwilsonlaw.com. You can get an answer from me directly by emailing trw@ryanwilsonlaw.com. Our office number is 240-638-2721.

RYAN WILSON

Elder Law Attorney
The Law Office of T. Ryan Wilson

Ryan Wilson is an experienced attorney in Silver Spring, MD. He is driven to provide expert legal advice, using the right legal tools to help his clients achieve their objectives. His practice includes elder law, estate planning, probate and trust administration, and small-business and nonprofit advising. Prior to opening his own firm, Mr. Wilson spent a number of years advising members of the Maryland General Assembly. He later worked with the financial services industry and regulators to protect the retirement savings of older Americans.

Ryan is a member of the Maryland State Bar Association (MSBA), where he is a member of the Section Council of the Elder Law and Disability Right Section. He is also a member of the MSBA Estate Planning and Real Property sections. Mr. Wilson is also an active member of the Montgomery County Bar Association, and he is a member of the State Bar of California.

Mr. Wilson is a member of the National Academy of Elder Law Attorneys (NAELA) and serves as Secretary of NAELA's Maryland/DC Chapter. Mr. Wilson is also a member of the Estate Planning Council of Montgomery County, Maryland. He serves as a member of the Montgomery County Commission on Aging.

WEBSITE:

www.ryanwilsonlaw.com

PHONE:

240-638-2721

EMAIL:

trw@ryanwilsonlaw.com

ABOUT THE PUBLISHER

Mark Imperial is a Best-Selling Author, Syndicated Business Columnist, Syndicated Radio Host, and internationally recognized Stage, Screen, and Radio Host of numerous business shows spotlighting leading experts, entrepreneurs, and business celebrities.

His passion is to discover noteworthy business owners, professionals, experts, and leaders who do great work and share their stories and secrets to their success with the world on his syndicated radio program titled "Remarkable Radio."

Mark is also the media marketing strategist and voice for some of the world's most famous brands. You can hear his voice over the airwaves weekly on Chicago radio and worldwide on iHeart Radio.

Mark is a Karate black belt; teaches Muay Thai and Kickboxing; loves Thai food, House Music, and his favorite TV shows are infomercials.

Learn more:

www.MarkImperial.com
www.BooksGrowBusiness.com

www.ingramcontent.com/pod-product-compliance
Lightning Source LLC
LaVergne TN
LVHW020047110826
845155LV00029B/674